Wisdom Beyond Measure

Wisdom Beyond Measure

The Sermon on the Mount

Donna Hughey

RESOURCE *Publications* · Eugene, Oregon

Resource Publications
An Imprint of Wipf and Stock Publishers
199 W. 8th Ave., Suite 3
Eugene, OR 97401
www.wipfandstock.com

ISBN 13: 978-1-62032-309-0
Manufactured in the U.S.A.

Contents

Introduction

THE SERMON ON THE Mount is probably the best known teaching of Jesus. Matthew 5–7 records this sermon in its entirety, although sections of it are scattered throughout the gospels. Jesus delivered the sermon early in his ministry to his disciples and to a large number of people who had gathered around him. He spoke to them from a hillside—one modern theory suggests this was a hill on the north end of the Sea of Galilee, while another suggests a hill between Capernaum and Tabgha. This latter hill, once known as Mount Eremos, is now the site of a Catholic chapel known as the Church of the Beatitudes.

The gospel of Luke records a similar sermon known as the Sermon on the Plain (Luke 6:17–49). It is considerably shorter than the sermon recorded in Matthew, and while both sermons share obvious similarities, they are not identical. Some biblical scholars believe this is the same sermon, and that Luke may have summarized the sermon while Matthew recorded it completely. Another view is that Luke may have relied on the writings of Mark—the first gospel written and used by churches—as his primary source for this information.

Regardless of the sermon's exact location or whether Luke and Matthew documented the same set of teachings, the main issue surrounding the Sermon on the Mount is how directly it should be applied to everyday life. Many believe the Sermon on the Mount contains the primary principles of being a Christian and that Christ gave the true interpretation of the laws of Moses; others claim portions of the sermon were exaggerated and should not be taken literally. Another popular idea is that Jesus was not giving specific instructions about how to *be* a Christian but instead offered general guidelines about how to *behave* as a Christian.

This sermon was not intended for unbelievers but for those who were already followers. Jesus sets forth a high standard, teaching that all Christians are to shine like a light so righteousness, ethical conduct, and love for others would be apparent to unbelievers. Believers are to be holy, different, and set apart from the world.

Because of the many debates surrounding the Sermon on the Mount, how are we to approach this study? At first glance, these teachings from Jesus seem impossible for a Christian to uphold. How are we to develop righteousness, turn the other cheek, or love our enemies? If we lack any of these characteristics, does that mean we are not true followers of Christ? It will serve us well to remember what Scripture teaches: a renewing of the heart, or rebirth, is essential before man can attempt the life-long process of achieving Christ-like behavior—further proof that man can accomplish nothing apart from God.

1

The Beatitudes

Matthew 5:1–6

Summary

THE SERMON ON THE Mount begins with the beatitudes (Matthew 5:3–11). The word "beatitude" derives from the Latin word *beatus* and is best translated as "happy" or "blessed." In this sense, the beatitudes explain who will receive blessings from God.

The first beatitude describes "the poor in spirit." These believers recognize their unworthiness before God. Being the deepest form of repentance, "poor in spirit" is an acknowledgement of total depravity and dependence on God. Only those who realize they have nothing to offer God, and who rely solely on his mercy for salvation, will receive, as a free gift, the kingdom of heaven.

The second beatitude describes "those who mourn." These are believers who recognize and grieve over their personal sin before God. They mourn for unbelievers and weep over a world that has rejected God. But they are comforted knowing that their sin is forgiven and that God redeems those who follow him.

The next beatitude describes "the meek," those who put humility into practice. These believers do not think more of themselves than their fellow man, and they put others' needs before their own. The meek understand they are citizens of the kingdom of God and are humbled to be shown his mercy.

The fourth beatitude describes "those who hunger and thirst for righteousness." These believers pattern their lives in agreement with the will of God. Believers who hunger for God and strive to conform to his principles will find satisfaction. This represents a cycle of growth among believers: the more we conform to God, the more attractive God becomes.

Getting the Basics

1. What will the poor in spirit inherit?

READ LUKE 17:20–21.

2.   What is the kingdom of heaven?

3.   What will those who mourn receive?

READ 2 CORINTHIANS 1:4.

4.   What does it mean to be comforted by God?

5.   What will the meek inherit?

READ 1 CORINTHIANS 3:21–23 AND 2 CORINTHIANS 6:10.

6.   What does it mean to inherit the earth?

7.   What will happen to those who hunger and thirst for righteousness?

READ EZEKIEL 28:5–9.

8.   According to verse 9, what does it mean to be righteous?

Digging Deeper

9.   Is it possible for a wealthy person to be poor in spirit?

READ 1 CORINTHIANS 3:22 AND 13:12; AND 1 JOHN 3:2.

10.   Do you believe that the blessings promised in the latter part
of each verse are attainable now, in the future, or both? Explain.

11. Why do you think studying the beatitudes causes discomfort among some believers?

12. What might these first four beatitudes teach a non-Christian?

Something to Think About: Our Relationship to God

The first four beatitudes deal with the believer and his relationship to God. To understand these beatitudes more fully, we must also understand God's relationship with the people of Israel. In Leviticus 18:1–4, God made a covenant with Israel after rescuing them from slavery in Egypt. He promised to be their God and that they would be his special people, living a different lifestyle than their neighbors and keeping his commands. But their devotion did not last.

Throughout the centuries following the covenant in Leviticus, the people of Israel began to mimic the practices of other nations around them. They rejected God, demanded an earthly king, and wanted to serve idols (1 Samuel 8:5–9). Many times God sent his prophets to remind Israel of who he was, but still they rejected him (2 Kings 17:7–17; Ezekiel 5:5–6). Because of this rejection, judgment fell on Israel and God gave them over to their sinful desires.

With this background in mind, Jesus is reminding the people on that mountaintop how deep their spiritual poverty ran. He tells them to be poor in spirit (to recognize they have nothing to offer God); to be mournful (to grieve over the gravity of their sin); to be meek (to see a true view of themselves); and to hunger and thirst for righteousness (to seek God). This process would restore them to their covenant with God.

These first four beatitudes are just as relevant to Christians today as they were to the Jewish crowd that Jesus addressed. Just as the Jews rejected God with their disobedience, we stand guilty before God with the same charge against us. We often forget the severity of our sin and fail to put God first in our lives. Within these beatitudes, we see the truth of who we are. Only through the power of a regenerated heart and the Holy Spirit can we begin to live a life of righteousness pleasing to God.

2

Transformation of the Heart

Matthew 5:7–12

Summary

THESE NEXT FOUR BEATITUDES focus on extending grace and forgiveness to others.

The first beatitude describes the "merciful." These are believers who forgive others because they recognize their own need for constant forgiveness by God. They forgive because they too are forgiven.

The second beatitude describes the "pure in heart." These are believers who are completely transparent before God and man. Their thoughts, motives, and actions are pure, and no hypocrisy or ulterior motives can be found within them.

The next beatitude describes the "peacemakers." These are believers who practice harmony in their relationships, in their churches, and in their communities. They avoid being the cause of conflict and strive to love all people just as God does.

The last beatitude describes "those who are persecuted." These are believers who are subjected to abuse by a world that has rejected God.

Getting the Basics

1.   What do the merciful receive?

READ 1 PETER 1:3-5.

2.   What does it mean to be merciful to others?

3.   What do the pure in heart receive?

READ PHILIPPIANS 4:8 AND 1 PETER 1:22.

4.   How would you describe a "pure heart"?

5.   What do peacemakers receive?

6.   What do the persecuted receive?

Digging Deeper

READ HOSEA 6:6; MATTHEW 9:9–13; AND ROMANS 12:1–2.

7. In what ways is mercy related to worship?

READ 1 JOHN 3:2–3.

8. What do you think it means to "see God"?

9.   How do you think a believer can achieve peace in his life?

READ JOHN 1:12–13 AND ROMANS 8:14.

10.   What does it mean to be called "sons of God"?

READ MATTHEW 5:12 AND 1 PETER 4:12–16.

11. How are we instructed to react when being resisted or opposed?

READ MATTHEW 5:3 AND 5:10.

12. Why do you think the first and last beatitudes promise the same reward?

13. Do you think Jesus provided the beatitudes as encouragement for us to improve our behavior, or as a way of showing us our failings as Christians? Explain.

Something to Think About: Christian Conversion

Christians react to the beatitudes in many ways. Some believe they are demands from God to be rigidly followed and think, "If I live like this, I will be a Christian." Others claim it's impossible and unrealistic to live a life the way Christ describes it here, so they ignore the beatitudes altogether. Still others pick and choose from the beatitudes, hoping to please God by adhering to a few of them. For a clearer understanding about how to apply them to our lives, we should first examine the beatitudes as a whole.

We begin this process by noticing there is a distinct order to the beatitudes. Each one is placed in the exact location so the next beatitude can build on it. Starting with spiritual poverty, Jesus teaches that we need to recognize we are sinners and that we deserve nothing but judgment from God. Once this condition is acknowledged, mourning and grieving over our sin takes place within our hearts. This grieving produces humility, an awareness that we are undeserving of God's grace, and a hunger for righteousness takes root in our hearts. This is the process of being born again. Every Christian experiences each step of the first four beatitudes at his conversion. Then, once the renewal of the heart takes place and the relationship with God is restored, the desire and ability to live a life pleasing to God becomes possible. We are now able to display mercy, godly motives, and harmony to those around us even while being insulted and persecuted for our change of heart.

When viewing this teaching as a whole, the beatitudes represent a kind of blueprint for a right relationship between God and man. The first part of each beatitude states the condition of *becoming* a citizen in God's kingdom, and the latter part describes the character of one who *has become* a citizen in God's kingdom. With this in mind, instead of thinking, "If I live like this, I will be a Christian," it may be best to think, "*Because* I am a Christian, I will live like this."

3

Living as Believers

Matthew 5:13–16

Summary

THESE VERSES FOCUS ON the responsibility of every believer to reflect God in today's society. Jesus uses salt and light as metaphors to illustrate how Christians are to demonstrate God's goodness and love in a corrupt world. In ancient times, salt had two important uses: as a preservative and for flavoring. Without it, food would spoil and be tasteless. Jesus, by talking about salt, teaches that all Christians must exercise the characteristics outlined in the beatitudes in both their actions and their words to help preserve goodness in society and to keep the world from rotting.

We are also told to be the light of the world. Jesus is implying that the world is shrouded in darkness and unbelief—but Christians can illuminate that darkness. Jesus builds on this using the example of a city on a hill. Although towns and villages in the lower valley are covered in darkness, the light from the city on the hill can be seen for miles around. In other words, Christians are not to hide who they are but boldly live out their faith for all to see. By doing so, their lives provide direction for those who are lost in a dark, corrupt world.

Getting the Basics

1. How might a believer be the salt of the earth?

2. What are some of the symptoms of a believer who has lost his saltiness?

3. How might a Christian, shining with good works, point an unbeliever towards God?

READ 1 PETER 2:12.

4. Ultimately, how does performing good deeds affect unbelievers?

Digging Deeper

READ LEVITICUS 2:13 AND EZEKIEL 43:24.

5.   How is salt connected with Old Testament sacrifices?

6.   What good is salt if it loses its flavor?

READ 2 CORINTHIANS 4:6.

7. What does the light that shines in Paul's heart represent?

8. What might cause a believer to hide his Christianity from others?

9. How might this negatively affect a believer's relationship with God?

10. If the church is supposed to be a light for God, do you think it has been successful or unsuccessful? Explain.

11. How might a believer benefit by publically displaying his faith?

Something to Think About: Demonstrating God's Truths

The apostle Paul goes into great detail about what happens to society when they reject the truth of God. He teaches that God will give them over to their sinful desires, resulting in utter deterioration and corruption (Romans 1:18–32). To halt this downward spiral, God tells Christians they are the salt of the earth, the ingredient to stop the decay of mankind. How is this accomplished? By living a life opposite of what a sinful world accepts. We are called to be different, set apart, and unashamed for all to see. By doing so, our unbelieving neighbors will see the goodness of God and he will be glorified.

A Christian can effectively demonstrate God's goodness and love to those around him in many different ways. One of the most successful methods is through living our lives truly dedicated to God. When we allow others to observe our honesty, good works, and desire to live a righteous life, the love of God naturally flows from us, and our neighbors and coworkers and even strangers will see the work of God firsthand.

Remember, the world is watching us with a critical eye. If our actions are not consistent with our words, then we have failed in showing others the love of God and failed in bringing glory to our father in heaven.

4

Old Testament Law

Matthew 5:17–20

Summary

AFTER USING THE EXAMPLES of salt and light, Jesus now teaches about Old Testament law. He states that he did not come to abolish the law but to fulfill it. There are several reasons why Jesus might make this statement. His audience may have mistakenly thought Jesus was opposed to the law since his interpretations differed from those of the Pharisees. They may also have been hoping Jesus was encouraging an overthrow of the law because of the rigid requirements placed on them by the Pharisees. In actuality, Jesus was not against the law at all. As a devout Jew, he honored it. His purpose for teaching about the law was to show that keeping to a set of strict rules and regulations was not enough to obtain true righteousness, and that one must have a change of heart to overcome sin.

Getting the Basics

READ ROMANS 7:7.

1. Why did God give the law to the people of Israel?

READ PSALM 19:7.

2. How does David describe the law?

READ GALATIANS 3:19–25.

3.   How does Paul explain the purpose of the law?

READ GALATIANS 2:16.

4.   Paul states that man is not justified by keeping the law. On what basis is man justified?

READ EZEKIEL 36:26 AND ROMANS 2:29.

5.   Although the scribes and Pharisees knew the law was good and tried to keep it, why were they struggling?

6.   Why must our righteousness exceed that of the Pharisees?

Digging Deeper

READ ACTS 10:9–33.

7. How is the clean and unclean law of the Old Testament fulfilled in Peter's vision?

READ JAMES 2:10.

8. What does this verse teach about breaking God's laws?

READ ROMANS 6:15–23.

9.   Some believers might think they can disregard the law now that they are saved by grace. Why is this incorrect?

10.   How should believers today respond to the law?

11. Do you believe the church is justified in applying new rules to its members? Explain.

READ ROMANS 6:14.

12. What does Paul mean when he says that we are not under law but under grace?

Something to Think About: Fulfilling the Law

Many Christians are confused about how Jesus fulfills the laws and commandments of the Old Testament. Because Jesus states he did not come to destroy or abolish the law, believers are left wondering why we don't practice the requirements of the Old Testament, such as observing the Sabbath or traveling to Jerusalem three times a year. To answer these and other questions, we must first look at the law itself.

Some biblical scholars divide the Old Testament law into three categories: the moral, the ceremonial, and the civil. The first category, moral law, includes God's holy demands for his people and is summarized in the Ten Commandments. The second category, ceremonial law, mainly refers to the sacrificial system, although it also includes food restrictions. The next category, civil law, contains the procedures and punishments of capital crimes, such as murder and adultery, for a nation ruled by God. But how did Jesus fulfill each of these categories?

Jesus fulfilled the moral law through his sinless life. Although he faced the same temptations we face, he obeyed the moral law completely and fully.

Jesus fulfilled the ceremonial law in ways that Aaron, the first high priest, couldn't. For example, Aaron entered the earthly tabernacle only once a year while Jesus entered the heavenly tabernacle for all time. Aaron also offered many sacrifices year after year while Jesus offered only one—himself. Lastly, Aaron offered sacrifices for his own sin while Jesus sacrificed himself for the sins of others.

Jesus fulfilled the civil law through his death on the cross, substituting himself in place of a sinful people who deserved death themselves.

While there is much debate about whether Old Testament law, in whole or in part, is binding for Christians today, Jesus sums up the whole Old Testament in Matthew 22:37–40 by saying, "Love the Lord your God with all your heart and with all your soul and with all your mind. This is the first and greatest commandment. And the second is like it: Love your neighbor as yourself. All the Law and the Prophets hang on these two commandments." By following and obeying these two commandments, believers display total devotion to God and love to their fellow man, thereby fulfilling both the moral and the social responsibilities within the Old Testament law.

5

Exposing Motives of the Heart

Matthew 5:21–32

Summary

JESUS NOW TEACHES HOW to manage anger, lust, and divorce. These relate to the sixth and seventh commandments given to Israel by God on Mount Sinai (Exodus 20:3–17). While Jesus doesn't add anything new to the Old Testament commandments, he does explain their true intent: to expose the motives and purity of the heart. By using the words "you have heard it said" in each application, Jesus is referring to the teachings of the Pharisees who had contaminated Scripture with false interpretations based on oral tradition. Jesus is not contradicting the Old Testament law which he previously validated, but instead he contrasts the interpretations of the law by the Pharisees with his own correct interpretation.

Getting the Basics

READ MATTHEW 23:25–28.

1. How does Jesus describe the Pharisees and teachers of the law?

READ GENESIS 4:1–8 AND EPHESIANS 4:26–27.

2. How are sin and anger related?

READ MATTHEW 5:23–26.

3. What instructions does Jesus give to a believer who has offended another?

READ DEUTERONOMY 24:1–4.

4. Under what conditions does Moses permit divorce?

READ MATTHEW 19:9; MARK 10:11–12; AND LUKE 16:18.

5.   How is divorce and adultery related?

6.   What exception does Jesus give for divorce in Matthew 5:32?

READ MATTHEW 5:29–30.

7.   In your own view, do you think Jesus is advocating a literal self-mutilation? Why or why not?

Digging Deeper

READ PROVERBS 14:17.

8.   What warning is given about the behavior of an angry person?

READ 1 JOHN 2:9–11.

9.   What attitudes are expressed in these verses?

READ JAMES 1:19–20.

10. How can anger lead to an unrighteous life?

READ MATTHEW 5:23–24.

11. Why do you think Jesus considered reconciliation more important than the act of worship?

12. In your own view, is there a difference between adultery and lust? Explain.

READ HEBREWS 13:4.

13.   What does this verse teach about the sexually immoral?

Something to Think About: Dealing with Anger

Getting angry is not always wrong, but we must recognize the difference between righteous and unrighteous anger. Righteous anger is an anger consistent with the righteous character of God. For example, John 2:13–16 describes Jesus clearing the temple of the moneychangers and animal-sellers with great emotion and anger. He was angry because the temple was a place of worship and prayer, not a place of profit and cheating. Also, Mark 3:5 describes how Jesus became angry at the Pharisees when they refused to answer his questions. His anger was due to his grief over the Pharisees' lack of faith.

In both cases, the anger Jesus displayed was a righteous anger—in other words, Jesus was angry for the right reasons. His anger wasn't due to personal insults against him or because of petty arguments. His anger had the correct focus: it was targeted towards sinful behavior.

Unrighteous anger, on the other hand, is an anger where selfishness is involved. Cain is a good example of unrighteous anger. Genesis 4 tells us about Cain's anger toward God and his brother Abel. Cain's anger was due to hatred and jealousy; because his anger was motivated by selfishness, it was out of control and resulted in the murder of his brother. Clearly, selfish anger must always be avoided.

Some people have an incorrect understanding of anger, thinking that all anger is sin and must be avoided at all cost. They show no emotion when Scripture, Christ, or God come under attack. Scripture does not teach us to suppress or ignore our anger; rather, it teaches that we are to deal with our anger properly and in a timely manner (Ephesians 4:26). So while anger in itself is not sinful, we can sin in reaction to it. Remember, Jesus did not succumb to man's selfish attitude when he was angry, but instead he displayed the righteous anger of God.

6

Oaths, Revenge, and Love

Matthew 5:33–48

Summary

IN THIS PASSAGE, JESUS instructs us to speak the truth and to keep our word. If we follow these instructions, our integrity will speak for itself. According to the Old Testament, people used oaths to seal agreements, resolve disputes, and affirm the truthfulness of important matters. They swore oaths in God's name only, knowing that to swear on God's name when a statement is false is a violation of the third commandment and punishable by death (Leviticus 24:10–16).

During the time of the New Testament, to avoid being found guilty of falsely swearing on the name of God, the scribes and Pharisees swore by everything *except* God. They thought they could avoid accountability for their false words and actions simply because they swore by heaven or Jerusalem, not God himself. This way of thinking allowed the Pharisees to decide for themselves which of their oaths were worth keeping and which could be safely ignored. Jesus addresses this error in Matthew 23:16–22 and teaches that all people should simply tell the truth.

Jesus also tells us to love all people even if they are evil (Matthew 5:44) and even if they are our enemies (Matthew 5:44). He lists several different offenses that a believer might be faced with—such as insult or extortion—and in each example he instructs us not to retaliate for the offense. Instead he tells us to love all people, whether good or bad, and by doing so we exhibit the characteristics of God.

Getting the Basics

READ MATTHEW 23:16–22.

1.   How did the scribes and Pharisees misuse their oaths?

2.   What does Ecclesiastes 5:4–7 teach about making vows?

Oaths, Revenge, and Love

READ LEVITICUS 19:12; NUMBERS 30:2;
AND DEUTERONOMY 23:21–23.

3.   What does each verse teach concerning oaths?

READ ROMANS 12:16–21.

4.   What does Paul teach about revenge?

READ LUKE 6:27–28.

5. List three specific ways we are taught to love our enemies.

READ ACTS 7:54–60.

6. What is your reaction to Stephen's dying words?

Digging Deeper

7. Do you believe Christians are prohibited from taking oaths to tell the truth in a court of law? Why or why not?

READ HEBREWS 6:13-18.

8. Why did God confirm his promise to Abraham with an oath?

9. Deuteronomy 19:15–21 summarizes Old Testament law regarding the punishment for false testimony or lying. What will the offender receive for his crime and how will this punishment affect the rest of the people?

10. What principles for justice are found in the phrase "an eye for an eye and tooth for a tooth"?

11. Why do you think Jesus teaches believers not to retaliate when wronged?

12. Paul was a persecutor of Christians before his conversion, yet the apostles forgave and accepted him without seeking revenge for his past actions. Have believers benefited by this act of kindness and if so, how?

Something to Think About: Christian Integrity

Here Jesus teaches a lifestyle of Christian integrity demonstrated by honesty, truthfulness, and love. While individuals have different definitions of integrity, *Christian* integrity is consistently displaying Christ-like behavior in every circumstance, reflecting an uncompromising devotion to godly thoughts and actions. But sometimes believers compromise God's principles with the principles of the world. To guard against this, believers must be trusted to tell the truth no matter what the cost, must be trusted even when no one is looking, and must keep their thoughts, habits, and motives pleasing to God.

Within this passage, Jesus gives us guidelines as to how our behavior and attitudes are to reflect the character of God. He uses extreme examples of how to respond when confronted with physical abuse (turn the other cheek); a civil law suit (give more than what the person is suing for); government oppression (do more than what is demanded); and those asking for our help (give them what they request). In each example, the principle of love is demonstrated and God's standard of righteousness is apparent.

But the most effective example of Christian integrity is the behavior of Jesus during his arrest, trial, and crucifixion. Not once did he lash out, abuse, or manipulate his enemies. By practicing these same standards, we can ensure we possess the characteristics and integrity of a follower of Christ.

7

Religious Acts

Matthew 6:1–18

Summary

UP TO THIS POINT, Jesus has taught his followers the ideal condition of a righteous heart and concludes his teaching with, "Be perfect, therefore, as your heavenly Father is perfect." But now, Jesus shifts gears. Instead of focusing on a righteous heart, he now teaches how to outwardly express this righteousness while performing religious acts. Giving to the needy, praying, and fasting were common public displays at this time, and Jesus uses these acts as examples to teach his followers the difference between seeking man's approval and approval from God. He explains that God will not reward those who perform religious acts for the purpose of impressing others, and he calls these people hypocrites. They pretend to be deeply spiritual, but their true motivation is to bring attention to themselves and has nothing to do with honoring God.

Getting the Basics

1. What does Jesus warn against in Matthew 6:2?

2. What is Jesus emphasizing in Matthew 6:3 when he commands, "Do not let your left hand know what your right hand is doing"?

READ LUKE 18:9–14.

3.   In this parable, what is the difference between the prayers of these two men?

READ MATTHEW 6:5–7.

4.   Why does Jesus criticize the hypocrites about their praying?

5.   What instruction is given for prayer in Matthew 6:7?

READ MATTHEW 6:16–18.

6.   How does Jesus describe the correct way of fasting?

7. How does Jesus describe the incorrect way of fasting?

8. What reward do the hypocrites receive in Matthew 6:2, 6:5, and 6:16?

9. What does Ecclesiastes 12:14 teach about God?

Digging Deeper

10. According to Acts 2:44–45 and Acts 4:34–37, public giving is not prohibited. How can we reconcile these verses with Matthew 6:1–4?

11. When is it proper for others to see our acts of giving? When isn't it proper?

12. Matthew 6:8 teaches that God knows our needs before we ask him. In light of this, what is the purpose of prayer?

13. Why is it necessary for Jesus to provide a model prayer for his followers in Matthew 6:9–13?

14. What is the cause of hypocrisy when giving to the needy, praying in public, or fasting?

15. Why might a Christian sometimes want to appear more religious that he really is?

16. How can we avoid this way of thinking?

Something to Think About: Correct Motivation

The heart of this message emphasizes the correct motivation for serving God. Whether it's fasting, prayer, or giving to the needy, Jesus teaches that outward religious acts are to glorify God, not bring attention to ourselves.

In New Testament times, the Pharisees were far more interested in impressing others with their religious devotion rather than humbling themselves before God. On the outside, they looked fine. They had long, religious-sounding prayers and carried themselves with dignity and holiness. But Jesus tells us that on the inside, they were full of hypocrisy and wickedness (Matthew 23:27–28). Their religious motivation was purely self-centered and had absolutely nothing to do with bringing glory, honor, and praise to God. Jesus called them hypocrites and ridiculed the way they turn their righteous acts into public performances.

It is easy for Christians to point fingers at the Pharisees and call them hypocrites—but just like the Pharisees, we can also make a show of our good deeds to impress those around us. Are we guilty of drawing attention to ourselves about how much money we give the church? Do we flaunt our knowledge of Scripture to look better in the eyes of those around us? When we pray out loud, are we more concerned with sounding "religious" than with actually speaking to God? Have we given Jesus any reason to call *us* hypocrites because of our pride, arrogance, and conceit?

In light of these questions, Christians should evaluate their true motivations when performing religious acts in public, because those who seek attention and applause have "received their reward in full" (Matthew 6:2). These believers will win admiration and praise from men—but not from God.

8

Godly Desires

Matthew 6:19–24

Summary

HERE JESUS TEACHES HIS followers about money and earthly riches, and about the differences between our own desires and God's desires. He explains that we should store our treasures in heaven where they will never rot, decay, or be stolen. He warns believers that it is impossible for a person to serve both God and money because a person can only be truly devoted to one or the other. He teaches that man must be devoted only to the Father so riches, ambition, and greed will never take the place of God in our lives.

Getting the Basics

1. According to verse 19, what happens to the treasures on earth?

2. According to verse 23, what will happen if your eyes are bad?

3.   What are the two masters mentioned in verse 24?

4.   What happens when we try to serve two masters?

READ 1 TIMOTHY 6:7–10.

5. What do these verses teach about those who have a love for money?

READ ECCLESIASTES 5:10–17.

6. What dangers are associated with wealth?

Godly Desires

READ 1 TIMOTHY 6:17–19.

7.   What do these verses teach about storing up treasures?

Digging Deeper

8.   How do you think Christians store treasures in heaven?

9. Do you think Jesus is teaching against us having valuable earthly possessions? Explain.

READ JOB 1:21 AND PROVERBS 23:4-5.

10. Why should Christians set their minds on God and not on earthly things?

11. List several "desires of the heart" that can contaminate a Christian's walk with God.

12. How do you interpret "the eye is the lamp of the body" in Matthew 6:22?

13. Explain how 1 Kings 18:21 agrees with Matthew 6:24.

Something to Think About: Devotion to God

This passage explains that we should be devoted only to God. We are often distracted by the things of this world, and as a result we fail to please and honor God. Scripture describes several individuals faced with a choice between God or personal gain, and we can clearly see the consequences of those choices.

Judas Iscariot is a prime example. Judas was personally chosen by Jesus as an original apostle (Mark 3:19) and traveled with Jesus for three years, listening to him speak and witnessing numerous signs and miracles. However, we learn that Judas was also greedy (John 12:5–6) and stole money from the apostles' moneybag—a clear sign that he placed his love for money over his devotion to God. He further displayed his greed when he willingly approached the chief priests and agreed to hand over Jesus for the sum of thirty silver coins (Matthew 26:14–16). He found no satisfaction, however, and he eventually hanged himself from a tree (Matthew 27:5).

Another example of greed is recorded in Acts 5:1–11, when the Christian church was still in its early stages. During this time, many followers of Jesus voluntarily contributed money and personal possessions to the apostles for distribution among the needy. Ananias and Sapphira, a husband and wife, sold a piece of property to contribute to this ministry and brought the money from the sale to the apostles. They conspired to keep a portion of the money for themselves and lied to the apostles about the true amount of money they had received. Because their love for money outweighed their devotion to God, they died instantly.

We can also learn from the rich young man who asks Jesus what he must do to inherit eternal life (Mark 10:17–25). Jesus, recognizing the young man's attachment to his wealth, tells him to go and sell everything he has and give it to the poor. The rich man, unwilling to give up his money, turns away. He chose his possessions over God.

In contrast to these examples is Abraham. When God commanded him to sacrifice his son Isaac, Abraham was willing to obey. This proved that Abraham held nothing more valuable than his devotion and loyalty to God, including the life of his child (Genesis 22:1–18). As a result of Abraham's obedience, God spared Isaac's life and called Abraham his friend (James 2:23).

Each of these examples teaches the consequences or rewards associated with devotion to God. Judas, because of greed, betrayed Jesus (Matthew 27:3–5) and then committed suicide after Jesus was condemned to die. Ananias and Sapphira also revealed their greed and that their devotion to God wasn't genuine—although they pretended to be wholly devoted, God knew their hearts and passed severe and immediate judgment. The rich young man proved through his actions that the price for following God was too high for him, and while his greed gave him financial security on earth, he lacked God's eternal security. Only Abraham displayed complete loyalty and devotion to God and because of this, he was greatly rewarded.

We can learn much from each of these examples. Jesus tells us that the heart can only serve one master—God or the desires of the world—and as believers, we must choose which is more important. We cannot have it both ways.

9

The Dangers of Worry

Matthew 6:25–34

Summary

HERE JESUS CONCLUDES HIS teaching about God and materialism and gives several reasons why man should not be anxious about earthly needs. In many cases, people tend to worry about tomorrow even when their present needs have been met. But Jesus explains that worrying about food, clothing, or other material possessions shows a lack of faith in God and causes man to rely on his own strength. Jesus teaches his followers to "seek first his kingdom and his righteousness" and by doing so, God will provide us with what we need.

Getting the Basics

READ MATTHEW 6:26–30.

1. Why is it unnecessary to worry?

The Dangers of Worry

2. After reading this passage, what do you think it means to "seek first his kingdom"?

3. What is Peter worried about in each of the following events and how did he react?

    Matthew 14:29–31—

    Matthew 16:21–23—

    John 18:10–11—

READ PHILIPPIANS 4:6.

4. How should we react to anxiety?

Digging Deeper

5. According to Matthew 6:30, worrying shows a lack of what?

6. What is the significance of Jesus using birds and flowers to illustrate how God provides for us?

The Dangers of Worry

READ PSALM 34:10.

7. What is promised to those who seek the Lord?

8. Why do you think Jesus tells us not to worry about the future?

READ LEVITICUS 26:14–17.

9. What reason does God give for withholding his blessings from his people?

READ DEUTERONOMY 28:1–6.

10. What reason does God give for providing blessings to his people?

Something to Think About: God's Kingdom

Believers often overlook the message at the end of this passage. We tend to concentrate on God's promise to provide for our daily needs rather than our responsibility to "seek first his kingdom and his righteousness." But what exactly is God's kingdom? For a clearer picture, it may help to compare God's kingdom with most kingdoms of the world:

1. Only by being born again is it possible to enter the kingdom of God (John 3:3–5), while most worldly governments require being born of parents who are all ready citizens or by passing a written test.

2. God's kingdom is not limited by borders, fences, or walls, but is in the hearts of people of all nations (Luke 17:21), unlike the nations of the world in which their territories are contained to a certain area.

3. God's kingdom has no military army, but a spiritual army (Ephesians 6:12), while worldly nations arm themselves with external military strength.

4. God's kingdom uses the "honor system" for collecting tithes and offerings, while worldly nations enforce taxes collected by the governments.

5. God's kingdom consists of all citizens being leaders appointed by God himself, while most worldly nations select a few citizens as leaders either by popular vote or by the government itself.

6. In God's kingdom, human life is secure from conception into eternity, while worldly nations generally secure human life from birth to death.

7. God's kingdom contains laws and commandments that never change (Matthew 5:18), while worldly nations constantly alter, delete, and add to their laws.

While the above list is not a complete contrast between God's kingdom and that of the world, it does provide clear differences between the reign of God and the reign of man. God's kingdom is unique and set apart, offering hope, security, peace, and love to its citizens. It is not a kingdom of words but of power (1 Corinthians 4:20) in the present day and in the future to come.

Many Christians are guilty of placing God's kingdom somewhere in the future, not realizing that it exists here and now. If we acknowledge that God is king, our thoughts and actions will mimic those of Christ—and then we can honestly say we "seek first his kingdom and his righteousness."

10

Hypocrisy

Matthew 7:1–6

Summary

HERE JESUS TEACHES HIS followers about the attitudes they should have toward fellow believers. He tells us not to judge, explaining how quickly man can see the faults of others and how blinded he is to his own. He instructs us to first deal with our own sin, and then we will be in a position to help others with theirs. Believers who do not follow these instructions—Jesus calls them hypocrites.

Next Jesus talks about discernment. He warns us not to carelessly present God's holy things to "dogs" or "pigs," people who ridicule, mock, or argue as a way of rejecting the truth of God. Because dogs were filthy wild animals who scavenged in the city dumps, and because pigs were unclean animals to the Jews, these were harsh words to describe the people whom Jesus wanted believers to avoid.

Getting the Basics

1. What does each of these represent in Matthew 7:3?

    Sawdust—

    A plank—

2. When is it okay to remove a speck from a believer's eye?

3.   When is it not okay?

4.   According to Matthew 7:3–4, what makes a believer a hypocrite?

5.   List several ways you have unfairly judged another person.

6.   How can you avoid this in the future?

Digging Deeper

READ MATTHEW 18:15-17.

7.   How is this form of judgment a thought-out procedure?

READ LUKE 18:9-14.

8.   Do you think Jesus would have labeled the Pharisee as a hypocrite? Why or why not?

9. Galatians 2:11–14 tells us of Paul confronting Peter about his hypocrisy. Do you think Peter was judged appropriately? Why or why not?

10. What is the difference between judging and holding someone accountable?

Hypocrisy

READ MATTHEW 7:6.

11. Some Christians use this verse as an excuse not to share the gospel
    with others. What do you think this verse actually teaches?

Something to Think About: Judging Others

"Do not judge, or you too will be judged" (Matthew 7:1).

This verse is well-known, but it is often misunderstood and misused. Many Christians quote this verse to avoid confrontation, to avoid responsibility for their actions, or to shift blame away from themselves. How should we view this teaching? Is Jesus implying that we should ignore the sins of fellow believers so we won't be found guilty of passing judgment? Are we forbidden from having an opinion or from saying anything about right and wrong?

Not at all. Because we have a tendency to exaggerate the faults of others while minimizing our own, Jesus teaches that we are in no position to judge others without first dealing with our sin. Only then can we clearly see how to help others with theirs. Our role should be as neither judge nor hypocrite but as loving Christians who, after examining and correcting ourselves, are able to offer genuine help to others. We cannot act maliciously or cruelly when correcting an error, even if what we say is biblically true. The purpose is to build up and draw the offender closer to God.

But now a new danger arises. Since we have been taught not to judge others and taught to love our enemies as ourselves, it is easy for Christians to go to the extreme and ignore the faults and sins of all people. But Jesus speaks of this in Matthew 7:6. If we have given someone plenty of opportunity to hear and respond to the truth and he insists on turning his back on Christ, then he has become a dog or a pig and the truth is meaningless to him. We must realize that sometimes hearts are hardened and doors are closed, and to impose God's truth on others is useless and sometimes harmful: useless because they do not recognize the value of God's truth, and harmful because our actions can cause rage and disgust against God. Only through discernment can we be sure whether to press forward or to shake the dust from our feet and move on.

The main point to remember is this: private evaluation of others is not forbidden, but outwardly judging someone's motives or intentions is dangerous because only God knows what is truly in another man's heart.

11

Persistent Prayer

Matthew 7:7–12

Summary

IN THESE VERSES, JESUS explains the importance of prayer. He uses the words ask, seek, and knock to demonstrate how believers should be active and persistent when approaching God with their needs. While he tells his followers that they will receive anything they ask from God, this promise is not unconditional. Jesus explains that God only gives *good* gifts to his children, implying that believers may, at times, ask for something that may be harmful to them.

How do believers distinguish between good requests and bad requests? Jesus seems to anticipate this question and provides an immediate answer: by doing to others what you would have them do to you. By following this instruction, believers will develop a heart that imitates the heart of God. Believers who are closer to God will produce prayers and requests that are more closely aligned with God's will. This results in God keeping his promise: everyone who asks also receives.

Getting the Basics

1.   What promise is given in this passage?

2.   What conditions must be met in order for God to grant a request?

3. Do you think this promise is limited only to spiritual requests? Why or why not?

READ 2 CORINTHIANS 12:8–9.

4. What request did Paul ask of God?

5.   How did God answer Paul's prayer?

6.   How does Paul respond to God's answer?

7.　What are some reasons God might deny a request?

Digging Deeper

READ 1 JOHN 3:22–23 AND 5:14–15.

8.　According to these verses, what demands must be met before receiving all that we ask from God?

9.   What actions from these people cause God to deny their requests?

10.   What can a believer conclude if his prayers and requests seem to go unanswered?

READ MATTHEW 7:12.

11. Jesus teaches believers to treat others as we would like to be treated. If we practice this instruction, what will become evident to those we interact with?

12. How does practicing "do to others what you would have them do to you" result in obedience of the Old Testament law?

Something to Think About: Seeking the Will of God

Jesus makes a startling promise in this chapter. He promises that whatever we ask for, we will receive. But we know, through our own personal experiences, this isn't always the case. Even Scripture lists several instances where requests aren't granted. In Exodus 33:18–23, Moses asks to see God with his own eyes, completely exposed and face to face. But God denies Moses his request. Instead, God allows Moses only a limited glimpse of his glory as he passes by. Another example is 2 Samuel 12:15–19, where David pleads with God to spare the life of his infant son. God does not grant David's request and the infant dies. The apostle Paul also tells us in 2 Corinthians 12:8–9 that he pleaded with God on numerous occasions to "remove the thorn in my flesh," but the request was never granted.

Why does God promise to give us whatever we ask for in Matthew 7:7 if he won't actually grant all our requests? James 4:1–3 answers this question: we do not receive because we ask with wrong motives. What are wrong motives? Wrong motives are anything that is not in line with the will of God. How can we possibly know the will of God? By practicing exactly what Jesus teaches in Matthew 7:12—do to others what you would have them do to you. By following this instruction, our hearts, minds, and actions will be more conformed to that of God's and our prayers will no longer be filled with selfish desires. We will begin to desire what God desires—to see things through his eyes. Our petitions to God will no longer focus on our immediate gratification but will focus more on seeking inner righteousness—which in turn will reflect the character of God to those around us.

Remember, God promises to give good gifts to those who ask him. If we are not receiving, it's time to ask ourselves what we're praying for, what our motives are, and if our desires are in complete agreement with God's. Only after self-evaluation can we boldly come before God in prayer to ask, seek, and knock and to confidently know, with absolute certainty, that God will keep his promise. John says it clearly in 1 John 5:14–15: "This is the confidence we have in approaching God: that if we ask anything according to his will, he hears us. And if we know that he hears us—whatever we ask—we know that we have what we asked of him."

12

Choices

Matthew 7:13–23

Summary

JESUS GIVES SEVERAL WARNINGS in these verses. He tells believers that a man can only follow one of two roads: the narrow road that leads to life, or the wide road that leads to destruction. He makes it clear that there are no other options. He also warns us about false prophets who will penetrate his church and tells us how to recognize them. But the most revealing statement by Jesus in this passage is how to gain eternal life: only by doing the will of God.

Getting the Basics

1. What are four distinguishing features of both roads in this passage?

2. How does Jesus describe the heart of a false prophet?

READ LUKE 13:22–30.

3.   Why will some people be denied admission into the kingdom of God?

READ 1 CORINTHIANS 4:5 AND PHILIPPIANS 1:18.

4.   In light of these verses, what is important when serving God?

READ ACTS 19:13−16.

5. How can acting on God's behalf without the correct motivation be dangerous?

6. According to Matthew 7:21, how does man gain entrance into the kingdom of heaven?

Choices

7. What do you believe is the main characteristic of a true follower of God?

Digging Deeper

READ GALATIANS 1:6–9 AND 1 JOHN 2:20–23.

8. What is taught in these verses that may help a believer recognize a false prophet?

READ 2 CORINTHIANS 11:14–15.

9. Why is it sometimes difficult for believers to recognize a false prophet?

READ MATTHEW 22:29 AND 2 TIMOTHY 3:16–17.

10. What can aid believers with recognizing the truth of God?

Choices

READ ROMANS 12:2.

11. Jesus teaches that those who do the will of God will enter heaven. According to Paul, what needs to take place within a believer before he can recognize the will of God?

READ MATTHEW 22:37–39.

12. How can practicing these two commands help Christians with renewing their minds?

Something to Think About: False Security

There are some who find security in their salvation simply because they went through all the motions of being a Christian—such as baptism, communion, and attendance in church. They are under the false illusion that these religious acts have somehow guaranteed them admittance into heaven. But we learn from this passage that Jesus will reject them with the words, "I never knew you. Away from me, you evildoers!" (Matthew 7:23) How is this possible? In truth, God will reject those who accept Christ verbally but lack moral obedience to him. They may have called him, "Lord, Lord," but they never submitted their lives and wills to Christ. It was just lip-service.

God knows the motivation behind every thought, deed, and action (Revelation 2:23), and while man is easily fooled, God is not. He is not impressed with our religious rituals or our traditional Christian words; rather, he looks for evidence of a true believer—one who strives for obedience and who follows God's will. This evidence includes growth and maturity in the Christian's life (Colossians 4:12), conforming our minds to that of God's (Romans 8:6), being thankful in all circumstances (1 Thessalonians 5:18), as well as being submissive to God (Hebrews 12:9). While these are just a few examples, the true mark of a Christian is the desire to know and live according to the will of God as revealed in Scripture. We should immerse ourselves in God's written word and pray that the Holy Spirit will transform us through the renewing of our minds, resulting in what is good, acceptable, and perfect—the will of God (Romans 12:1–2). While it is true that man is saved only through Jesus Christ by God's grace, it is equally true that obedience is a product of that grace.

13

Christian Security

Matthew 7:24–27

Summary

AS PART OF HIS conclusion, Jesus explains the consequences for hearing his words but not putting them into action. He compares our decision to follow him as a house built on a solid foundation, and he warns that hearing the truth and doing nothing leads to disaster. After talking about the narrow and wide roads, he again offers us a choice: security or catastrophe. He leaves each man to choose for himself.

Getting the Basics

READ MATTHEW 7:24 AND 26.

1.   What two choices are given in these verses?

2.   What do the rock and sand each represent in these verses?

READ 1 JOHN 1:6–7.

3. What do these verses teach about following Christ?

4. What does it mean for us that the house fell with a great crash in Matthew 7:27?

Digging Deeper

READ JOHN 15:5.

5. How does this verse agree with the parable of the house and foundation?

READ JAMES 1:25.

6. What is the reward for hearing and obeying God's word?

7. Some Christians ignore some of God's teachings, such as giving to the poor or tithing. Why do you think they do this?

8. How is it dangerous to read the Bible and attend church but not practice any of God's teachings?

READ ROMANS 10:17; 2 TIMOTHY 4:7; AND 1 CORINTHIANS 15:2.

9.   How can a Christian be sure he has built a strong foundation?

READ JOHN 14:15, 21, AND 23.

10.   Why do you think love is linked to obedience in each of these verses?

Something to Think About: Obedience and Disobedience

Christians should take notice of the warning given in this passage. Because we profess to be followers of Christ, we belong to the group of "hearers" that Jesus is describing. Our attendance in church, reading the Bible, and joining Bible study groups has exposed us to God's truth and the responsibility that goes with it—obedience. God hates disobedience from his followers because it shows a lack of trust in God to decide what is best for our lives. Man offers countless reasons for being disobedient to God but most are motivated by fear, personal pleasure, the desire for praise, or preferring our own wisdom over God's. When we disobey God's word, we attack God's glory and honor, and Jesus calls us foolish (Matthew 7:26).

On the other hand, obedience motivated by faith delights God. Although we may feel fear, weakness, or disadvantage, Scripture proves that believers with obedience motivated by faith accomplish the extraordinary (such as Moses, Joshua, David, Esther, Abraham, and Peter). Jesus calls these individuals wise (Matthew 7:24). This passage tells us that there will be storms in our lives and our victory depends on the foundation we choose to stand on: ourselves or God.

Conclusion

"When Jesus had finished saying these things, the crowds were amazed at his teaching, because he taught as one who had authority, and not as their teachers of the law." (Matthew 7:28–29)

THE SERMON ON THE Mount was delivered before the Christian church had been established. It was addressed to Jews who were followers of Jesus and who had witnessed his amazing miracles. The prophets, John the Baptist, and Jesus himself declared that the kingdom was at hand, and the idea of having a king who eliminated every sickness and who was capable of feeding them was very appealing. As a result, many Jews followed Jesus (Matthew 4:25). The problem, however, was that they were not spiritually prepared for the kingdom Jesus described.

The purpose of the sermon was to describe and teach the righteousness believers needed to qualify for entrance into the kingdom. Jesus intended his words to convict and condemn, revealing the depth of man's sin in much the same way as the Old Testament law (Romans 3:20). Jesus made it clear to the Jews that righteousness is not found in themselves, as they had been taught by their religious leaders (Matthew 5:20), but found only through him (Matthew 6:33). This truth is stated at the beginning of the sermon within the first beatitude (Matthew 5:3), teaching that those who recognize their spiritual poverty are in a position to acknowledge their need for a savior. In this sense, his words were also meant to encourage the faith of the hopeful.

The Sermon on the Mount teaches that man must have a regenerated heart before he can possess the *desire* or *ability* to live a godly life. This can only take place if one is willing to allow God to transform his heart, mind, actions, and behaviors to mimic those of Christ. This transformation is a life-long process and doesn't end until the believer stands in the presence of God. There will always be mistakes made and improvements needed on this life-long journey, but through Jesus Christ, believers are given strength, hope, courage, and power to live lives that reflect the Sermon on the Mount. Praise be to God forever and ever!

www.ingramcontent.com/pod-product-compliance
Lightning Source LLC
Chambersburg PA
CBHW060414090426
42734CB00011B/2309